RAILWAY MANUAL
(WAR).

120
___
Mobn.
264

1911.

(Reprinted, with amendments, 1914.)

The Naval & Military Press Ltd

in association with

The Imperial War Museum
Department of Printed Books

Published jointly by
The Naval & Military Press Ltd
Unit 10 Ridgewood Industrial Park,
Uckfield, East Sussex,
TN22 5QE England
Tel: +44 (0) 1825 749494
Fax: +44 (0) 1825 765701
www.naval-military-press.com
www.military-genealogy.com
www.militarymaproom.com

and

The Imperial War Museum, London
Department of Printed Books
www.iwm.org.uk

3

CONTENTS.

(B 11089) A 2

ABBREVIATIONS.

A.D.A.S.	...	Assistant Director of Army Signals.
C-in-C.	...	Commander-in-Chief.
D.A.D.R.T.		Deputy Assistant Director of Railway Transport.
D.D.R.T.	...	Deputy Director of Railway Transport.
D.R.T.	...	Director of Railway Transport.
F.S.R.	...	Field Service Regulations.
I.G.C.	...	Inspector-General of Communications.
L. of C.	...	Line or Lines of Communication.
Q.M.G.	...	Quarter-Master-General.
R.T.O.	...	Railway Transport Officer.

CHAPTER I.

OBJECT IN ORGANIZING THE RAILWAY TRANSPORT SERVICE.

1. *General Conditions.*

1. Every war in which railways have played an important part has emphasized the necessity for a military controlling authority.

2. Broadly speaking there are three different conditions under which railways will be utilized on service :—

   (i) Where the actual working is left in the hands of a friendly administration which is allowed to carry on its civil traffic as in peace time, so long as precedence is given to military requirements.

   (ii) Under conditions similar to the above except that the state of the country or the attitude of the civil population necessitate military control of civil as well as military traffic.

   (iii) In a hostile or disaffected country where it becomes necessary to replace the civilian working personnel by a military organization.

In all the above mentioned cases a military controlling organization is necessary apart from the working personnel.

3. The general principles governing the control, maintenance, and administration of railways in war are stated in F.S.R., Part I, Chapter III, "Movements by Rail," and in F.S.R., Part II, Chapters III and VIII. In this manual are given more detailed instructions as to execution of these services.

4. In ordinary circumstances military requirements will be met by the daily delivery at railhead of a number of men, and quantities of supplies and stores which will not greatly vary from day to day, and by the evacuation of sick and wounded. The railway arrangements necessary for these services present no special difficulties.

When, however, the additional movement by rail of masses of troops from one locality to another is in question, the requisite arrangements cannot be completed in an expeditious and satisfactory manner unless some notice of the proposed operations is given to the railway transport establishment.

5. So delicate and complex a matter is railway management that the efficient operation of a railway system can only be assured when the cordial co-operation of the railwaymen is combined with the strictest obedience of regulations by the troops.

The regular flow of traffic, for instance, may be easily upset by the use of locomotive water supplies for drinking purposes, of permanent way and other materials for the defence of buildings, by delaying trains beyond the scheduled time of starting or altering the composition of trains at the last minute. These and similar instances of interference, though at times unavoidable in war, require careful regulation by the military controlling organization.

6. Again in war rolling stock is required for ambulance trains, armoured trains, repair trains and private inspection carriages; all these demands, added to the inevitable losses and damage that must occur when the railway system runs through the theatre of operations, may form a serious tax on the resources of the line, and require careful regulation.

It is therefore necessary to secure the free circulation of rolling stock of all classes, and it is impossible for the railway personnel to get the full capacity out of the line unless the army co-operate in the matter of loading and unloading trains.

CHAPTER II.

THE RAILWAY TRANSPORT PERSONNEL.

2. *General Duties.*

1. The main duties of the personnel of the railway service may be summed up as follows :—

   (i) To be the intermediaries between the army and the technical administration of the railway.

   (ii) To see that the ordinary working of a railway is carried on in such a manner as to ensure the greatest military efficiency.

   (iii) To see, on the other hand, that the demands of the army on the railway, which must always be addressed through the Railway Transport Establishment, are, subject to military exigencies, so regulated as not to disorganize the working of the railway system as a whole.

2. Of these the third is of great importance, for it can be easily understood that the officers of a civil railway administration are not in a position to discriminate between the demands of the various branches and departments of the army, nor can they class them in any definite order of urgency.

It is therefore necessary to centralize the control of the railway and to prevent its unauthorized use by individual officers whose actions, the result of which they themselves are unable to foresee, may cause serious delay if not a positive breakdown.

3. The staff of the C.-in-C., of subordinate commanders, and of the I.G.C. will be kept informed, as required, by the Railway Transport Establishment as to the extent to which the railway system is equal to meeting military demands for railway transport required under the varying conditions of the campaign.

3. *Duties of Director and of Deputy Director of Railway Transport.*

1. The duties of the D.R.T. are defined in F.S.R., Part II, Section 24.

2. The headquarters of the D.R.T. will be located as decided by the C.-in-C.

It will usually be on the L. of C. when its position will be decided by the I.G.C.*

3. For the repairs and maintenance of the permanent way and works, the railway companies, R.E. are under the orders of the D.R.T., and if additional labour is required this will be provided under instructions from the I.G.C.

---

* At the date of issue of this Manual the D.R.T. is at G.H.Q., and reports directly to Q.M.G., E.F.

4. In the case of new railways constructed during operations, of railways taken from the enemy, and of railways whose previously existing personnel is for any reason not made use of, the D.R.Ts. duties include the provision of all material and personnel, and all arrangements necessary for the efficient maintenance and working of such lines. For this purpose a specially organized corps will be placed under him, which will include a suitable proportion of skilled men for each operating branch of a railway organization, and will be supplemented by civil and unskilled labour as circumstances demand.

5. The existing personnel and organization of railways in the theatre of operations will always be left undisturbed when such a course is consistent with their reliable and efficient working, and in these circumstances the D.R.T. will exercise only so much control as is necessary to ensure that the requirements of the army and of the military situation are properly met. His powers in this respect will be determined by the I.G.C., and must vary according to the circumstances of the campaign.

6. The D.R.T., under instructions from the I.G.C., makes the necessary arrangements with the civil administration of a railway for the conveyance of troops and material, and for settling the rates and fares to be paid for all kinds of military traffic.

The procedure for accounting for all such traffic and the methods of payment to the administrations concerned are also matters for settlement by the D.R.T.

The exact financial system and method of accounts must depend on which of the conditions described in para. 2, section 1, hold good.

7. A D.D.R.T. may be appointed to represent the D.R.T. either at General Headquarters or at the headquarters of the I.G.C. as circumstances may require. In the first case he will act as adviser to the staff; in the second he may be assigned all or any of the duties allotted to the D.R.T. in the preceding paragraphs.

4 *Duties of Deputy Assistant Directors of Railway Transport.*

1. At the principal railway centres on the L. of C. the D.R.T. is represented by D.A.Ds.R.T, whose duties are confined to certain sections or areas of each railway system.

Within this area the D.A.D.R.T. exercises a general control over all military traffic. The extent of control to be exercised over civil traffic must vary with the circumstances of the campaign, and is a matter for settlement as occasion may demand by the I.G.C.

2. The D.A.Ds.R.T. will keep the D.R.T. informed of the railway requirements on the sections to which they are posted, and will render to the D.R.T. such returns as may be required.

3. In conjunction with the railway officials they will arrange all troop movements which they are ordered to carry out and should personally supervise the entrainment and despatch of any large body of troops.

4. In the case of railways worked by a civil personnel, their further duties and powers will be fixed by the D.R.T., and must depend on the extent of control exercised as stated in paragraph 5, Section 3.

5. At important stations and junctions the D.A.D.R.T. is assisted by a R.T.O., whose chief duties are to supervise entraining and detraining at these stations, and generally to facilitate the transport of troops, animals and material.

6. R.T.Os. will be distinguished by a badge worn on the left arm marked R.T.O.

7. D.A.Ds.R.T., assisted by R.T.Os., form the railway transport establishment under the D.R.T., and except when fighting is imminent or in progress they will receive orders only from the D.R.T. or the D.D.R.T.

5. *Duties of a Railway Transport Officer.*

1. The military authority of a R.T.O., whatever his rank may be, will, as regards the movements of troops and their accessories by rail, be paramount at the station where he is posted for duty.

2. In matters of discipline and sanitation at the railway station where he is posted, the R.T.O. is responsible that the orders of the administrative commandant of the area are properly carried out, and he will be provided by the administrative commandant with the necessary police for this purpose.

3. He will superintend all entrainment and detrainment of troops at his station; detailed instructions regarding this are given in Chapter IV.

4. He will make himself acquainted with all particulars of the station and goods yards at which he is posted, their shunting and marshalling capacities and platform accommodation.

He must obtain accurate knowledge of the various patterns of carriage and wagon stock in use on the railway with their capacities for transport of men, horses, baggage, vehicles and military stores of all kinds, and with the composition of trains for the different units. For the capacity of certain types of rolling-stock see Appendix I.

5. It is his duty to supply the administrative commandant and other commanders with such information regarding the railway as they may need in connection with movements contemplated.

It will not usually be possible for the R.T.O. to acquire a knowledge of the general traffic and carrying capacity of the line, and such information must be sought from the D.A.D.R.T.

6. The R.T.O. will furnish the railway official in charge with all warrants for troops and their baggage entraining at his station, and in certain cases with carriers' notes and vouchers for stores; the procedure is given in detail in Chapter V.

7. He will be in close touch with the railway executive officials, but must not interfere with them or their subordinates in matters of

technical detail ; it is his duty only to explain clearly what is required to be done, leaving the manner of execution to them.

8. It is his duty to see that :—

(i) The efficient working of the railway is not adversely affected by any action on the part of the troops unless such action is necessitated by the exigencies of the military situation.

(ii) That rolling stock is loaded to the fullest extent permissible under the railway regulations.

(iii) That trucks are not kept under load at destination except with permission from the D.A.D.R.T.

(iv) That the regulations as to the use of railway buildings, water supplies, and railway material by troops are observed.

CHAPTER III.

TECHNICAL ORGANIZATION.

6. *Organization and Duties of Technical Personnel.*

1. The organization and duties of the military controlling authorities as described in Chapter II, will be the same whether the railways are actually worked by a civil personnel or by the special corps referred to in Section 3, paragraph (4).

2. In the latter case the organization and duties of the principal officers of the military corps will be, generally speaking, as follows :—

(i) The general manager, under the D.R.T., is responsible for the efficiency of the railway and its working.

He will be assisted by the following heads of departments, whose duties are as follows :—

(ii) The traffic manager controls all the arrangements concerning the collection, handling and delivery of traffic. He controls and directs the railway personnel whose duty it is to receive, forward and deliver the traffic, and is, therefore, responsible for :—

(*a*) Proper recording and invoicing of traffic received.
(*b*) Receipt of carriers' notes and warrants.
(*c*) Issue of tickets and receipts for goods.
(*d*) Accounting to chief railway accountant for traffic delivered.
(*e*) Tracing of traffic.
(*f*) Loading, unloading and checking of traffic.
(*g*) Handling of the traffic when loaded into trains.
(*h*) Marshalling rolling-stock into trains.
(*i*) Despatch and receipt of trains.
(*j*) Time tables and the crossing and handling of trains *en route.*
(*k*) Working of all stations with their signals and telegraphs.*
(*l*) Discipline and administration of the traffic personnel.

(iii) The locomotive superintendent is responsible for :—

(*a*) Specifications and design and erection of new locomotives, rolling-stock and machinery.
(*b*) Construction and working of the workshops of the railway, both in connection with the rolling-stock and in the output

---

* The telegraph operators and signalmen are under the orders of the traffic manager. The responsibility for construction, repairs and maintenance of railway telegraphs rests with the Director of Army Signals who will be represented by an A.D.A.S. attached to the headquarters of the D.R.T. for this purpose.

of work required from shops by engineering department. If, however, the engineering work is of any magnitude, the latter department would have their own shops, and only send to the locomotive superintendent such work as, from the want of proper machinery, they were unable to carry out themselves.

(c) Provision and working of the locomotives in accordance with traffic arrangements.

(d) Examination and repair of all locomotives and rolling-stock in use on the railway.

(e) Erection of coaling stages and locomotive watering plant.

(f) Discipline and administration of the personnel employed upon the above duties.

(iv) The superintending engineer is responsible for :—

(a) Survey, construction and maintenance of formation level, permanent way, bridges, signals, buildings and works of all kinds.

(b) Discipline and administration of the personnel employed upon these works.

(v) The chief railway accountant's duties are :—

(a) To record correctly all expenditure under the heads and subheads laid down by the general manager.

(b) To receive and account for all money due to the railway.

(c) To pay all bills, payment for which is duly authorized.

(d) To furnish statements of the accounts of the railway.

(e) To furnish statistics desired by the general manager.

(f) To control the accountants attached to each of the railway departments, to frame regulations for their instruction, and carry out internal audit of their accounts.

(g) To inspect and audit the accounts of station masters when revenue is received.

(h) To clear accounts with any adjoining railway system.

(i) To be responsible for the discipline and administration of his subordinates.

(vi) The chief railway storekeeper is responsible for :—

(a) Purchase and custody of all stores requisitioned by the heads of railway departments and the custody of all railway stores captured.

(b) Distribution of stores and their issue to such railway officials as are authorized to requisition and receive them.

(c) Accounting to the auditors for the stores received by him.

CHAPTER IV.

Movements by Rail.

7. *Traffic Arrangements.*

1. In the case of all normal traffic, arrangements should be such that the demands once fixed are met as far as possible automatically.

2. By normal traffic is meant the steady flow of supplies and material, drafts and reinforcements from the bases to the front.

3. Thus a fixed daily tonnage of trucks should be allotted by the I.G.C. to each administrative department, at the base and at distributing centres ; each department will be responsible that full and proper use is made of the allotted tonnage, and must endeavour to maintain a uniform output and to restrict abnormal demands as much as possible.

4. The space to be allotted daily in passenger trains for troops and details should be similarly fixed, but in their case it will not be possible to secure the same degree of uniformity.

5. Up to the limits of tonnage and train space thus fixed by the I.G.C., heads of departments and commanding officers will address their demands direct to the R.T.O. who will arrange with the railway.

6. When the needs of the army have thus been provided for, it is for the D.R.T. to say whether the capacity of the line necessitates restrictions on civil traffic, and if so what total tonnage and train space can be allotted to it.

7. The allotment of this total for civil requirements, will be made by the I.G.C., the D.R.T. being responsible only that the former officer's orders are carried out and for reporting to him if the tonnage and train space are not used for the purpose for which they are allotted.

8. To maintain a uniform flow of normal traffic should be the primary object of the railway personnel, but abnormal movements are inevitable and must be provided for.

9. In the term abnormal movements are included concentrations or movements on a large scale with little or no previous warning.

Such movements will almost always restrict normal traffic and will probably cut off entirely for the time being the flow of supplies over the sections of the line affected.

10. When considering the detailed arrangements for such movements, the following factors must be taken into account :—

    (a) When a movement of troops on a large scale by rail is contemplated which involves the carriage of horses and vehicles, it is necessary that the railway transport personnel should have preliminary notice giving the entraining stations and the numbers to be moved, even though the actual destination or the time at which the move will commence is not known.

On well equipped lines, such as those in Great Britain, approximately 24 hours preliminary notice is necessary to enable the railway to collect rolling stock and commence marshalling the trains.

After 24 hours for such preparation, the railway should be able to commence despatching trains within four hours of receipt of orders.

On Colonial lines it may be necessary to give 48 hours preliminary notice or even more.

Where there are no horses or vehicles to move, but only personnel and baggage, the entrainment of troops becomes a comparatively simple matter and four or five hours preliminary notice will generally be ample.

(b) The units of a division at war strength require in all 100 trains, including 24 different train compositions. It is therefore most important to have adequate facilities for marshalling trains within easy distance of the entraining stations ; unless there is a separate marshalling yard it is best not to attempt marshalling at entraining stations themselves. It is quite sufficient if the marshalling station is within one or two hours run and has good telephonic communication with the entraining station.

It is not always possible to foretell the exact order in which all the units will entrain ; but before commencing the move the railway officials must be given a list of the total rolling-stock required and the staff of the marshalling yard should have all the train compositions ; the R.T.O. at the entraining station must keep the latter advised of at least the next four or five compositions required, and such compositions once ordered must not be altered at the entraining station.

(c) The proportion of the total amount of rolling stock to be collected will, of course, depend on the time required to get stock returned from destination for a second trip ; when stock of a certain class is scarce it will be necessary to spread out as much as possible the units using that class, e.g., if cattle trucks are scarce, trains for cavalry and artillery should alternate with infantry trains so as to allow time to get the cattle trucks returned.

(d) In calculating the number of trains that can load and unload at a station simultaneously, one line through the station should always be left clear (except at terminal stations), and also sufficient room for shunting ; but, subject to the above, both up and down platforms should be used simultaneously.

(e) On double lines of rail the actual journey is seldom an important factor in the movement ; but on single lines, unless working to a fixed time table which is seldom possible, the normal time required may be doubled or trebled owing to returning traffic, and it is therefore desirable either to collect sufficient stock for the whole move or to return empties by another route no matter how circuitous such route may be.

11. The following example shows roughly the time required for a given move by road or rail :—

A division at war strength is to be moved 60 miles and it is assumed that roads exist by which the force could cover this distance and complete the move in 84 hours, *i.e.*, 4 days and 3 nights.

To move this force by rail would require in England about 2,400 trucks and carriages of various sorts, equivalent to at least 100 trains. If shunting facilities for marshalling trains and platform accommodation admit of marshalling one train per half-hour and placing three in position for loading simultaneously, thus giving about $1\frac{1}{2}$ hours per train for loading, then loading will be complete in 50 hours ; add 3 hours for the journey of the last train and 1 hour for unloading, and the whole operation will be completed in 54 hours.

If the distance to be traversed is reduced to two days' march, say 30 miles, the time required to complete the operation by road is reduced to 36 hours while the train journey will still take $52\frac{1}{2}$ hours.

In the above example of a 60 miles journey it would probably take 12 hours to get stock returned and ready again for loading, so that about 30 per cent. of the 2,400 vehicles should suffice, but if artillery and mounted troops all entrain consecutively a larger proportion of cattle trucks would be needed.

12. It must, however, be remembered that of the 2,400 railway vehicles required in the above example about 1,578 are for artillery and ammunition columns, and transport and supply columns and park.

By making these portions of the troops march the railway requirements are reduced to about 30 trains, most of which are for infantry which can entrain and detrain quicker and with fewer facilities than are required for mounted troops and transport.

13. It follows from the above considerations that to expedite railway moves, care should be taken in selecting entraining and detraining stations ; an extra day's march to a suitable station may easily save 48 hours in entraining a division, and similar advantage may be gained by entraining and detraining at two or more different stations simultaneously.

14. Except on emergency or under very exceptional circumstances troops must never entrain or detrain on the line outside stations.

Responsibility in carrying out Movements.

1. The extent to which D.A.Ds.R.T. and R.T.Os can arrange abnormal movements of troops or material without reference to the D.R.T. must vary with the circumstances; their powers in this respect should be defined as far as possible by the D.R.T. and published in orders so that commanders and departments may know to whom to address their demands and thereby save delay.

2. Decentralization in this respect is essential if unexpected movements of troops and stores are to be carried out rapidly. On the other hand, D.A.Ds.R.T. and R.T.Os. cannot be allowed to arrange train movements the effects of which on other sections of the railway system they are unable to foresee and which may have a prejudicial result on the military traffic as a whole.

3. The above remarks apply equally to the technical personnel of the railway, in that it is desirable that district traffic officers and station masters shall be in a position to carry out movements ordered by the D.A.D.R.T. or R.T.O., without having to refer to the headquarters of the railway.

4. In peace, under normal circumstances, trains have to run punctually in accordance with working time tables, involving a considerable degree of centralization; in war time it is desirable to relax this as much as possible, and it is a matter for the D.R.T. to arrange with the managers of the railway systems concerned for a greater degree of latitude to be given, if necessary, to their district officers and station masters.

5. When active operations are in progress in the vicinity of the railway, R.T.Os., or in their absence the railway personnel, must immediately act on the order of a responsible officer suspending traffic owing to the approach of the enemy. On every occasion of such suspensions the R.T.O. will report the circumstances through the D.A.D.R.T. to the D.R.T. Officers who order or authorize such suspensions must recognize that they incur a grave responsibility and must report their action and reasons therefor to their superior officer with the least possible delay.

9. Entrainment and Detrainment of Troops.

1. Instructions for troops moving by rail and for entraining and detraining personnel, animals and stores are given in F.S.R., Part I.

2. At stations where entrainment takes place on any large scale a suitable place of assembly is necessary in close proximity to the station; troops must not enter station buildings or occupy any platforms until their respective railway vehicles or trains are in position ready for loading.

If the place of assembly is some distance from the station, telephonic communication between them should be established.

3. Administrative commandants in consultation with L. of C. defence commanders and R.T.Os. will select and prepare suitable places of assembly, the necessary arrangements for latrine accommodation and drinking water for troops at places of assembly being made by the administrative commandant.

4. When troops are ordered to move by rail the R.T.O. will obtain from the branch of the staff concerned the necessary authority for the moves and the following information :—

Place of entrainment and destination.

Strength of each unit in (1) officers ; (2) N.C.Os. and men ; (3) 2-wheel vehicles ; (4) 4-wheel vehicles ; (5) guns ; (6) weight and description of baggage ; (7) animals.

Date and approximate hour at which the move is to commence.

5. The R.T.O. having made the necessary arrangements with the railway will notify the staff of :—

(i) Time at which baggage, guns, vehicles or animals and fatigue parties for loading should be at the place of assembly.

(ii) Hour of departure of train or trains.

(iii) Halts on the journey for food or rest.

(iv) Probable time of arrival at destination.

The information being given for each unit of the force to be moved.

6. In the case of movements ordered at short notice, where rolling-stock has to be collected hastily, it will not generally be possible to supply the above information for all units before the move commences. R.T.Os. should, however, give each unit as much warning as is possible of its time of departure.

7. Dismounted troops without baggage should not arrive at the place of assembly more than half-an-hour before the time of departure ; 15 to 20 minutes in their case is sufficient time for entraining.

8. The R.T.O. should see that officers in charge of units or advanced parties are shown :—

(i) Place or places of assembly.

(ii) Entrances into the station to be used.

(iii) Platforms where baggage, animals, &c., are to be loaded.

(iv) Platforms where troops are to entrain.

(v) Allotment of vehicles to the unit.

The advanced party, if time permits, should mark on each vehicle the baggage, animals, &c., to be loaded in it, or the number and description of troops it is to carry.

9. It is not the duty of the R.T.O. to issue detailed orders regarding the entrainment or detrainment of units, or regarding their discipline and arrangements during the journey ; but he is responsible for bringing to the notice of commanding officers any special railway regulations which it is necessary the troops should know.

10. *Despatch of Stores and Animals.*

1. In the case of stores or material consigned by rail from small depôts and not accompanied by troops, the administrative commandant on application from the R.T.O. will detail such fatigue parties as may be required for loading and unloading.

2. At the base and at the principal despatching and receiving depôts, where the despatch and receipt of stores is continuous, directors of administrative services will organize their own labour supply for loading and unloading.

3. The authority consigning animals will be responsible for loading them up and will detail attendants for the animals *en route*, and will arrange that sufficient forage for the journey is loaded with them.

4. Troops travelling by rail are responsible for loading and unloading all baggage, animals and transport of their units.

CHAPTER V.

WARRANTS AND FORMS TO BE USED.

11. *Troops, Baggage, Animals and Transport.*

1. When applying to the railway transport establishment for railway transport or train accommodation, the commanding officer or individual concerned should produce the order of an officer authorized to order such movements.

2. To save misunderstanding on the part of the railway transport establishment the designation of officers authorized to order movements should be published in standing orders.

3. Orders authorizing movements may be written or telegraphed. In the absence of such orders R.T.Os. have power to refuse to allow troops or individuals to travel by rail.

4. The following paragraphs apply in all cases where detailed payment has eventually to be made for railway transport for any part of the journey.

5. The order or authority referred to in paragraph 3 must be supplemented by a travelling warrant or forwarding note, which is the railway's authority for providing the necessary accommodation, and which eventually becomes their voucher for the recovery of the necessary charges.

6. Travelling warrants will normally be issued by officers of the railway transport establishment ; at stations where there is no such officer, the post commandant will issue warrants for individuals and details who can be accommodated in the ordinary train service. Where extra accommodation is required he will apply to the nearest R.T.O.

7. Authority to issue travelling warrants on L. of C. for a limited number of troops will be given to other officers only under authority of the I.G.C., the designations of such officers and the extent to which they may issue warrants should be notified to the D.R.T.

8. Officers authorized to issue travelling warrants will apply for the necessary warrant forms to the D.R.T. who is responsible for their preparation and issue.

Should such officers have to entrain individuals or troops at stations where there is no R.T.O., and when they have no warrant book with them, they will hand the station master a written requisition for the accommodation required stating the numbers of personnel, animals, transport and stores to be carried. The station master will, as soon as possible, apply to the nearest R.T.O., who, after verification, will give him a warrant in proper form in exchange for the written requisition.

9. The forms of warrant used will vary in accordance with the arrangements made by the D.R.T. with the railway administrations concerned regarding rates, &c.

10. The ordinary forms of warrant used for railway journeys in England are shown in Appendix II for reference ; slight modifications may be necessary to adapt them to service conditions, and it may be advisable to have a combined form of warrant both for troops and baggage.

11. In Appendix II is also given a suitable form of warrant for use when a vehicle rate is in force. This form of warrant will be used only by officers of the railway transport establishment.

12. The regulations as to the use of warrants contained in the King's Regulations will be observed as far as possible, but the route form prescribed in the King's Regulations for use in peace will not be used in war.

13. An officer in charge of warrant books on being relieved will hand them over to his successor.

14. Officers when issuing warrants will be careful to inform the persons to whom they are issued that they must be presented at the booking office of the station where the journey commences and exchanged for a railway ticket, otherwise the holder will be liable to pay his fare when tickets are collected at the termination of the journey.

15. Separate warrants should be made out for conducting parties for whom return tickets are required, or when it is necessary to obtain a cheap ticket for a portion of any journey, or in any other circumstances in which a saving can be effected thereby.

16. Before issuing a warrant for the homeward portion of a return journey, the issuer should ascertain whether a return warrant was originally given. If so, a report should be made immediately to the payer of the warrant, in order that a double charge may be prevented.

17. The number and particulars of the warrant issued will be entered on the authority referred to in paragraph 1.

When the applicant can produce no such authority, the R.T.O. or other officer, if he decides that circumstances justify the issue of a warrant, will report to the C.O. of the unit concerned the number and particulars of the warrant issued.

18. The approximate weight of guns and military transport wagons should be given except when they are booked at vehicle rates.

19. Appendix II also shows the purposes for which the various forms of warrants are to be used.

12. *War Department Stores.*

1. The procedure to be adopted and the forms to be used when stores are conveyed by rail are described in the A.S.C. Training, Part III.

2. The term stores as used above includes only supplies and material not yet issued and not forming part of the equipment of a unit.

3. At stations where there is no representative of the Director of Transport, R.T.Os. will carry out their duties in all matters respecting the consignment of stores by rail. It is therefore the duty of R.T.Os. to make themselves acquainted with those portions of A.S.C. Training, Part III, which apply to the carriage of stores by rail, and with any modifications thereof published in Standing Orders.

4. The despatch by rail of baggage accompanying troops will be carried out on active service by R.T.Os. or officers authorized to issue warrants.

5. Under the term baggage are included all stores, supplies and material issued to or forming part of the equipment of a unit, and such private property as the unit is authorized to carry on service.

13. *Advices and Returns of Movements by Rail.*

1. The submission of daily or periodical returns should be restricted as much as possible, and only such returns should be called for as are likely to serve some definite and useful purpose. Those enumerated in paragraph 9 of this section will probably suffice.

2. Should the circumstances under which the returns or advices were originally called for, alter to such extent as to render them no longer of use, or no longer of use in their existing form, they should be immediately discontinued.

3. All officers of the railway transport establishment are responsible for bringing the facts to the notice of their superiors should it become clear that circumstances have changed since a particular return was called for.

4. It is especially important to restrict advices and returns sent by telegram, and care should be exercised by all concerned to restrict the use of the wires to messages of urgency or importance.

5. Under normal conditions R.T.Os. will wire the following advices in the case of individuals and troops entraining at their stations :—

(1) To the R.T.O. or station master at the station where troops next halt for food, information as to the meals required and probable hour.

(2) To the R.T.O. or station master at next station where troops have to change carriages, information as to numbers and ultimate destination, in order that accommodation may be arranged for in advance.

(3) To the R.T.O. or station master at the next station where troop or special trains have to be re-marshalled or split up, information as to the composition of each train and

contents, ultimate destination and probable hour of arrival, in order that the composition in which trains will go forward may be arranged.

(4) To the R.T.O. at final destination, or if there is none to the D.A.D.R.T. of the district in cases where troop and special trains go right through, information as to the composition of each train, contents, probable hour of arrival and such other information as may be necessary in order that the R.T.O. or the D.A.D.R.T. at destination can make proper arrangements for detraining.

6. To the D.A.D.R.T. under whom he is serving, the R.T.O. will only wire information regarding any abnormal traffic with which he is concerned. The precise nature and extent of such information is a matter for settlement by the D.A.D.R.T.

7. A similar rule should apply regarding information wired by D.A.Ds.R.T. to the D.R.T., the principle being that only so much information shall be wired as is necessary in order to keep D.A.Ds.R.T. and the D.R.T. informed of the progress of abnormal traffic movements.

8. Returns of the total despatches of stores and material from the bases and principal supply depôts will be a matter for the departments concerned.

9. Returns of such despatches will, as a rule, only be required from the railway transport establishment in order to see that vehicles are quickly and economically loaded at despatching stations, and at receiving stations to see that trucks are not kept unduly long under load.

The form of return should be arranged so as to show :—

(i) Number of trucks placed at disposal of each administrative service or department daily or weekly, their total tonnage capacity, and, if possible, their cubic capacity.

(ii) Actual weight of stores loaded or total cubic contents.

(iii) Average time trucks are detained for loading or unloading.

CHAPTER VI.

AMBULANCE AND ARMOURED TRAINS.

14. *Ambulance Trains.*

1. The D.R.T. will arrange for fitting up ambulance trains, and for their maintenance in good order.

2. At stations where hospitals are established it is necessary to provide a special siding, as near as possible to the hospital, in order that the hospital train, which can only be emptied slowly, may not hamper other traffic.

15. *Armoured Trains.*

1. The functions of armoured trains are described in F.S.R., Parts I and II.

2. The D.R.T. will arrange for their construction and maintenance and for the necessary railway personnel for working them.

3. Armoured trains have the right to demand precedence over other traffic, but are bound equally with ordinary trains by the usual rules of working, such as in leaving or entering stations or block sections. They must not leave a station without obtaining the line clear ticket order, staff, tablet, or starting signal as the case may be. They must not enter a station against the signals or run past opposing signals anywhere. When there is no urgency they take their turn with other trains ; when, for good reason, they exercise their right to claim precedence, it is the duty of the traffic officials to clear the line for them as speedily as possible, and to let them into or out of stations with the least possible delay. Armoured trains must be allowed to use the railway telegraph wires and to attach telephones, phonopores or telegraph instruments to them, under general working regulations agreed to by the A.D.A.S. and the traffic manager.

Armoured trains should not remain on a section blocking the passage of other trains except for very urgent reasons, and when so doing the officers commanding should get into telegraphic communication with stations on either side to keep them informed of their intentions. Armoured trains should as a rule keep moving ; when not required they should halt only at places well provided with siding accommodation.

4. The crew of an armoured train includes, besides combatant troops, the personnel necessary for driving the engine, executing small repairs to the train and minor repairs of damage to the

permanent way and telegraph caused by the enemy. This railway personnel is provided by the railway departments concerned with the work ; thus the locomotive superintendent provides engine driver and fireman, the traffic manager provides a guard and telegraphist, the superintending engineer provides platelayers, the A.D.A S. provides lineman. These heads of departments replace casualties and provide reliefs when necessary, but the personnel on the train are not under their orders after they have been handed over to the officer commanding the train, who will be under the commander of L. of C. defences.

5. The engines and rolling-stock are constructed and kept in repair by the locomotive superintendent and inspected by his subordinates from time to time. The locomotive superintendent is responsible that the armoured trains are in a fit condition to run, and for the withdrawal and replacement of any locomotive or vehicle not in a condition to travel safely.

16. *Expedients necessary in War.*

1. When the line is threatened by the enemy, it may be necessary to adopt expedients in the making up of trains which would be considered hazardous in ordinary working. For instance, whenever it is considered possible that the enemy may have interfered with the line, at least one and preferably two or three heavily loaded trucks should be placed in front of the locomotives of the trains travelling over a section which has not been used quite recently. If possible, trucks in front of the locomotive should be. bogies. Where trains are heavy and gradients steep and long, the trains proceed so slowly that the enemy may be able to ride up and pull off the vacuum pipe at the back of the brake van and so bring the train to a standstill. It will be necessary in such cases to attach a truck in rear of the brake van with its pipe uncoupled, the risk of such a truck becoming uncoupled and running away being less than the risk of the enemy stopping the train. It may also be necessary on the most dangerous sections to put an armoured truck containing a small garrison in the centre of the train, and to have brake vans armoured and loop-holed. Instructions concerning these special measures should be conveyed to the railway *employés* through their superiors, in order that they may know when they may or may not depart from the usual rules of railway working.

CHAPTER VII.

CARRYING CAPACITY OF RAILWAYS.

17. *Information necessary to estimate Capacity.*

1. Any estimate of the maximum carrying capacity of a railway for military purposes, if based only on statistics or framed by persons not actually connected with its management, should be accepted with great caution.

2. There are many factors in the question which can only be known to the officials actually employed in the management of the line who alone are competent to give reliable figures.

3. As a guide to officers who may have to report upon the capacity of a line and its vulnerable points, a form of report is given in Appendix III, which shows the various points upon which information is necessary.

It would not be possible to obtain all this information except with the assistance of the railway administration concerned.

4. Where such assistance is not forthcoming, the following information must be got from actual observation in addition to such information as is published in reports or statistics :—

(i) Entraining and detraining facilities for men, animals, vehicles and stores at the principal stations. A sketch of the station with brief explanatory notes is the best form of report. Where this cannot be done give :—

(a) Length, breadth and height of each platform, stating whether it is on the main line or on a loop or siding, and whether there is convenient access for vehicles and animals from the neighbouring roads on to the platforms.

(b) Length of each siding with and without platform accommodation.

(c) Nature and size of ground in station yard or vicinity suitable for forming up troops and transport for entraining or detraining.

(d) Supply of drinking water available.

(e) Area of shed accommodation available for stores stating whether it is alongside a siding or otherwise.

(f) Crane power (travelling or stationary) available for loading or off-loading heavy stores.

(ii) Number of trains worked each way daily, speed and usual number of vehicles on goods and passenger trains respectively, stating whether vehicles are 4-wheelers or bogies. Published time-tables, which do not usually include goods trains, are not of much use for ascertaining numbers, but are of use in arriving at the speed of trains.

Where, as is often the case, the traffic varies greatly over different portions of the line, the information should be given separately for the different sections.

(iii) Sizes and carrying capacity of the different types of goods and passenger vehicles.

(iv) Number and distance apart of stations, and of crossing stations on single lines.

(v) Number of lines of rail (single, double, treble, &c.), gauge, weight of rail, &c.

5. In estimating the loads of trains for military stores it must, however, be remembered that the cubic capacity of trucks, and not the maximum load which they can carry, is usually the ruling factor.

6. A statement of the approximate bulk per ton of military material is given in Appendix IV.

From Appendix I it will be seen that certain types of British covered wagons allow about 62 cubic feet per ton, and open wagons loaded to a reasonable height allow about 55 cubic feet per ton. With stores bulkier than this full loads cannot be obtained.

7. In estimating how far the normal carrying capacity could be increased and the additional stock, plant, &c., that would be required, the following basis of calculation may be used :—

The loads of troop and material trains and their speeds having been arrived at from the above data, the total train-miles per diem to work a given volume of traffic can be determined.

To arrive at the amount of stock required for this traffic it may be assumed that an engine can average 60 miles a day ; the work of passenger and goods stock must vary with local conditions, but it is seldom safe to assume more than 120 and 50 miles respectively per day throughout the year, including repairs. For short periods of say six months these figures can be increased by 50 per cent.

8. Fuel and water supplies are matters of great importance in calculating how far traffic can be increased in countries with little water and coal resources.

An average figure would be misleading as it must vary 100 per cent. or more according to the gradients and state of the roads, the condition of the engines and stock, and, of course, the nature of the fuel.

The following figures are the results obtained by one of the principal English railways and will serve as data on which to base an estimate. It may be assumed that the coal used in these tests was good steam coal and that the engines were in the best order.

Where wood fuel only is obtainable its coal equivalent must be ascertained. In India $2\frac{1}{2}$ lbs. hard wood fuel is taken as equal to 1 lb. Bengal steam coal.

Water consumption will vary even more largely and in the absence of any reliable data at least 70 gallons per train-mile should be allowed for to cover everything.

SUMMARY OF WORKING OF ELEVEN COMPOUND 8-WHEELED COUPLED GOODS TENDER ENGINES.

Period.	Engine Hours.		Goods Train Detentions.		Goods Train Miles, from Guard's Road Notes.	Goods Train and Engine Miles, from Driver's Return.			Ton-Miles.	
	Hrs.	Min.	Hrs.	Min.		Train.	Assisting, Shunting, &c.	Total Engine Miles.	Total Ton-Miles.	Average Tonnage per Train-Mile.
12 months ending November, 1909	24,411	37	4,895	34	132,284	132,280	64,364	196,644	63,743,133	481

Period.	Total Coal Used.	Less for Detentions, 3 Cwts. per Hour.	Net for Traction.	Average Consumption of Coal in Lbs.			Pints of Oil Used.			Average Consumption of Oil per—		
	Lbs.	Lbs.	Lbs.	Per Train-Mile.	Per Engine-Mile.	Per Ton-Mile.	Oil Loco.	Oil Cylinder.	Total Oil Used.	100 Train-Miles.	100 Engine-Miles.	100 Ton-Miles.
12 months ending November, 1909	13,334,060	1,644,984	11,689,076	88·36	59·44	·183	9,284	9,059	18,343	13·86	9·32	·0288

SUMMARY OF WORKING OF ELEVEN SIMPLE 8-WHEELED COUPLED GOODS TENDER ENGINES.

Period.	Engine Hours.		Goods Train Detentions.		Goods Train Miles, from Guard's Road Notes.	Goods Train and Engine Miles, from Driver's Return.			Ton-Miles.	
	Hrs.	Min.	Hrs.	Min.		Train.	Assisting, Shunting, &c.	Total Engine Miles.	Total Ton-Miles.	Average Tonnage per Train-Mile.
12 months ending November, 1909	27,459	9	4,868	45	114,690	114,830	85,867	200,697	55,020,961	479

Period.	Lbs. of Coal Used.			Average Consumption of Coal in Lbs.			Pints of Oil Used.			Average Consumption of Oil per—		
	Total Coal Used.	Less for Detentions, 3 Cwts. per Hour.	Net for Traction.	Per Train-Mile.	Per Engine-Mile.	Per Ton-Mile.	Oil Loco.	Oil Cylinders.	Total Oil Used.	100 Train-Miles.	100 Engine-Miles.	100 Ton-Miles.
	Lbs.	Lbs.	Lbs.									
12 months ending November, 1909	14,130,448	1,655,605	12,194,843	108·94	62·25	·227	9,006	7,805	16,811	14·65	8·37	·0305

APPENDIX I.

CAPACITY OF BRITISH ROLLING STOCK.

Description of Stock	Dimensions (inside).	Cubic capacity.		Load.	Average cubic feet per ton.	Remarks.
		Actual.	If loaded to a height of 5 feet.			
Open goods wagon, L.N.W.R.	15' 6" × 7' 2" × 3' high....	Feet. 333	Feet. 555	Tons. 10	55	
,, ,, L.S.W.R.	14' 11⅜" × 7' 6¼" × 2' 11⅞" high	337	562	10	56	
Covered goods wagon, L.N.W.R.	17' 9¼" × 7' 1" × 6' 11½" high at centre	807	621	10	62	

APPENDIX I—*continued.*

When journeys exceed eight hours, the numbers of men given herein should be reduced by one-fourth.

ENGLISH ROLLING STOCK—CAPACITY FOR TROOP MOVEMENTS.

Nature of Vehicle.	Clear width inside.	Clear length inside.	Clear height inside.	Door opening.	Remarks.	Capacity for Military Transport.
Covered goods wagon, bogie ...	7' 4½"	32' 10½"	6' 3"	6' 0" high, 5' 0" wide	No windows or louvres	Not suitable for men owing to lack of ventilation; not suitable for vehicles, suitable for stores requiring protection; will take 30 tons.
Goods wagon, 10-ton, converted for sheep truck (four-wheel)	7' 2" inside posts	15' 6" except at corners	2' 0" to top of side of truck, 4' 0" to top of frame	4' 10" wide	These frames, converting the trucks into cattle wagons, can be quickly put in or taken out	Will take 6 horses, saddled or unsaddled; can take 20 men crowded or 10 tons stores; not suitable for vehicles.
Goods wagon, open, 10-ton (four-wheel)	7' 6"	15' 6"	2' 0" to top of side	Whole side lets down	... ...	Very suitable for vehicles (see Appendix V for dimensions of vehicles). Will take 10 tons stores or 21 men crowded; not suitable for horses.
Goods wagon, open, 8-ton (four-wheel)	7' 2"	14' 7"	2' 1½"	Ditto	... ...	Load 8 tons of stores; very suitable for vehicles (see Appendix V for dimensions of vehicles). Will take 19 men crowded; not suitable for horses.

Iron covered goods wagon (four-wheel)	7' 5"	15' 11½"	5' 8½"	4' 10½" wide	Not sufficient ventilation to enable troops to be carried ...	Carries 9 tons of stores; suitable only for goods; very suitable for explosives.
Cattle wagon (four-wheel) ...	7' 2½"	18' 0"	6' 8¾"	4' 0" wide	...	Will take 7 horses saddled or 8 unsaddled, or, if necessary, 8 tons stores.
Twin timber wagon, consisting of two four-wheel wagons	7' 3¼"	31' 1", each wagon 15 0" with 1' 1" interval	...	...	Flat cars with no sides or ends, a bolster with side bars in the centre of each four-wheel wagon	Suitable for rails or timber; not suitable for vehicles, but could be used provided vehicles are scotched and lashed. Load for a twin wagon 20 tons.
Open goods wagon, bogie ...	7' 6¼"	34' 1½"	2' 8½" to top of side	Whole side lets down	...	The most suitable wagon existing for military transport; will take vehicles (see Appendix V for dimensions of vehicles), or will take 46 men crowded or 25 tons stores. Could, if necessary, be converted for horses with framework similarly to four-wheel wagons.
Covered goods wagon (four-wheel)	7' 1"	17' 9½"	5' 10½"	5' 10" wide	...	Not suitable for men owing to lack of ventilation; not suitable for vehicles; suitable for stores requiring protection; will take 10 tons.

PASSENGER COACHES.

Each compartment will hold 8 men with their kits, but they will not be able to sleep. With 5 men to a compartment, they can take it in turn to sleep 3 at a time. The number of compartments in a coach varies from 5 to 8.

APPENDIX I—continued.

IRISH ROLLING STOCK—CAPACITY FOR TROOP MOVEMENTS.

Nature of Vehicle.	Clear width inside.	Clear length inside.	Clear height inside.	Door opening.	Remarks.	Capacity for Military Transport.
Standard four-wheel carriage trucks	7' 0"	14' 6"	1' 5¾"	End-loading	… … …	Suitable for vehicles, or will take 16 men crowded or 4 tons stores.
8-ton four-wheel covered wagon	6' 9"	14' 6¾"	5' 4"	4' 4"	No ventilation for troops …	Not suitable for men; will take 8 tons stores.
End-loading wagon (four-wheel)	7' 2¾"	18' 1½"	11¾"	Ends fall down	… … …	Very suitable for timber, rails, and vehicles, or would take 24 men crowded or 8 tons stores.
10-ton four-wheel coal wagon …	7' 8"	16' 0½"	2' 8"	4' 6"	Could be converted into cattle wagons in the same way that is done with English sheep trucks	If converted into cattle wagon, would take 6 horses saddled or 7 horses unsaddled, or will take 10 tons stores or 22 men crowded.
Four-wheel falling-side wagon…	7' 8"	16' 0½"	1' 6"	Whole side (falls down)	… … …	Very suitable for vehicles, or would take 8 tons stores or 22 men crowded.
Covered cattle wagon	7' 2¾"	13' 9¾"	6' 3½"	4' 4"	… … …	Will take 5 horses saddled or 6 horses unsaddled. A horse box takes 3 horses.

Passenger coaches 10 men to a compartment, usually 6 compartments in a coach.

Canadian Rolling Stock.

Nature of Vehicle.	Clear width inside.	Clear length inside.	Clear height inside.	Door opening.	Remarks.	Capacity for Military Transport.
C.P.R. 65' 0" 1st class carriage (bogie)	9' 2¼"	65' 0" over frame	...	...	Lighted with acetylene gas, heated with pipes, two smoking rooms	Takes 48 1st class passengers.
C.P.R. 60' 0" 1st class carriage (bogie)	9' 2¼"	60' 0" over frame	...	...	Lighted with acetylene gas, heated with pipes	Takes 67 1st class passengers.
C.P.R. 72' 0" tourist carriage (bogie)	9' 2¼"	72' 0" over frame	...	...	Lighted with acetylene gas, heated with pipes, also kitchen and smoking room	Takes 56 passengers.
C.P.R. commissary carriage (bogie)	9' 2½"	56' 0" over frame	...	...	Two store rooms, kitchen has four fires, five ovens, two boilers. Tank below.	
C.P.R. 67' 0" colonist carriage (bogie)	9' 2½"	67' 0" over frame	...	...	Lighted with acetylene gas, heated with pipes, kitchen on each car	Takes 72 passengers.
C.P.R. 50' 0" horse carriage (bogie)	8' 5½"	50' 0" over frame	6' 6"	5' 0" wide	Fitted with trough, mangers; horses travel parallel to length of truck	Take 16 horses unsaddled, or 12 horses saddled.
C.P.R. 30-ton stock carriage (bogie)	8' 8"	36' 0"	7' 1¼"	Ditto	Fitted with feed racks ...	Take 16 horses unsaddled or 14 saddled.
C.P.R. 30-ton goods box carriage (bogie)	8' 4¼"	35' 0"	...	Ditto	... ...	Will take 30 tons of stores; would require to have windows cut before using for troops, would then take 53 men. If fitted with bunks would take 24 men sleeping.
Ditto ditto 40-ton ...	8' 4¼"	36' 8"	...	Ditto	... ...	Ditto ditto, load 40 tons.

C

APPENDIX 1—continued.

CANADIAN ROLLING STOCK—continued.

Nature of Vehicle.	Clear width inside.	Clear length inside.	Clear height inside.	Door opening.	Remarks.	Capacity for Military Transport.
C.P.R. 30-ton flat carriage (bogie)	9' 0"	35' 0"	No sides or ends	...	... ...	Suitable for vehicles when lashed or scotched, also for rails, timber, &c.; load 30 tons.
Ditto ditto 38' 8" long (bogie) ...	9' 0"	38' 8"	Ditto	...	... ...	Ditto, ditto.
C.P.R. 40-ton flat carriage (bogie)	9' 0"	36' 8"	Ditto	...	... ...	Ditto, ditto; load 40 tons.

SOUTH AFRICAN ROLLING STOCK.

Nature of Vehicle.	Clear width inside.	Clear length inside.	Clear height inside.	Door opening.	Remarks.	Capacity for Military Transport.
C.S.A.R. low-sided open goods truck (Z.A.S.M.)	7' 1½"	19' 4¼"	2' 9¾"	5' 0"	Four-wheeled truck, sides do not remove or let down	Takes 10 ton of stores; not suitable for vehicles. Takes 25 men.
Ditto ditto, another type ...	7' 1½"	24' 7¼"	2' 9¾"	5' 0"	Ditto	Ditto ditto, but takes 32 men.
C.S.A.R. twin bolster truck (Z.A.S.M.)	7' 4½"	11' 8"	...	...	No sides or ends, each portion of twin truck is four-wheeled	Suitable for rails or timber, load 20 tons on the two.
C.S.A.R. platform bogie wagon (Z.A.S.M.)	7' 0"	37' 0"	Ends 1' 6", side stanchions 3' 6"	All stanchions removable, along whole length	...	Load 20 tons, very suitable for rails, timber, or vehicles; similar wagon (P.P.R.), takes 55,000 lbs.

35

					Four-wheel truck	
C.S.A.R. high-sided open goods truck (Z.A.S.M.)	7' 1½"	24' 7¼"	5' 7" ...	5' 0" ...	...	Can be used for animals, load 10 tons; takes 32 men.
C.S.A.R. short covered goods truck (Z.A.S.M.)	7' 1½"	19' 5½"	...	...	Ditto ...	Suitable for ammunition or stores requiring care, not suitable for troops unless ventilation provided; load 10 tons.
C.S.A.R. open cattle wagon (Z.A.S M.)	7' 1½"	19' 5½"	5' 3"	5' 0"	Ditto ...	Takes 8 horses, load 10 tons.
C.S.A.R. low-sided bogie (P.P.R.)	7' 2"	37' 8"	2' 4"	Whole side lets down	...	Very suitable for men, vehicles or baggage; takes 49 men; load 55,000 lbs.
C.S.A.R. covered cattle wagon (P.P.R.)	7' 2¼"	19' 6¼"	...	5' 0"	Four-wheel	Takes 8 horses.
C.S.A.R. low-sided short goods truck (O.V.S.S.)	7' 3"	18' 4"	2' 3"	Whole side lets down	Ditto ...	Suitable for vehicles, baggage, or men, load 10 tons; takes 24 men.
C.S.A.R. low-sided bogie goods truck (O.V.S.S.)	7' 3"	36' 10"	2' 0½"	Ditto	...	Excellent vehicle for military traffic, very suitable for vehicles, baggage, and men, load 40,000 lbs.; takes 49 men.
C.S.A.R. sheep truck (O.V.S.S.)	6' 11"	18' 4"	3' 0"	5' 6"	Four-wheel	Suitable for baggage, or can be fitted to take 8 horses, load 10 tons; takes 23 men.
C.S.A.R. covered cattle wagon (O.V.S.S.)	7' 1"	15' 5"	7' 1"	5' 0"	Four-wheel	Takes 7 horses unsaddled, or 6 saddled.
Ditto ditto, another type	7' 3"	18' 0"	7' 0"	5' 0"	Ditto ...	Takes 8 horses unsaddled, or 7 saddled.
C.S.A.R. high-sided iron bogie open goods truck	7' 0"	37' 0"	3' 2"	6' 0"	...	Not suitable for vehicles, load 60,000 lbs.; will take 52 men. Could be fitted to take animals.
Ditto ditto, another type	7' 9"	37' 0"	3' 8"	6' 0"	...	Ditto ditto, but load 70,000 lbs.
Ditto ditto, another type	7' 9"	35' 0"	4' 0"	8' 0"	...	Ditto ditto, but load 70,000 lbs. or 49 men.

APPENDIX I—*continued.*

SOUTH AFRICAN ROLLING STOCK—*continued.*

Nature of Vehicle.	Clear width inside.	Clear length inside.	Clear height inside.	Door opening.	Remarks.					Capacity for Military Transport.
N.G.R. high-sided bogie goods wagon	7′ 3″	36′ 1″	3′ 1½″	4′ 0″	...	...	...	...	...	Load 20 tons or 47 men.
N.G.R. low-sided bogie goods wagon	7′ 3″	38′ 2″	1′ 7½″	Whole side lets down	...	...	...	...	...	Very suitable for vehicles, load 20 tons or 47 men.
N.G.R. also possess six-wheel and four-wheel goods wagons and iron bogie trucks, the latter very similar to C.S.A.R. trucks of that type. N.G.R. cattle wagons hold from 17 to 19 horses.										
Cape Government railway rolling stock is very similar to C.S.A.R. types (O.V.S.S.) and to the iron bogie stock of C.S.A.R.										

SOUTH AFRICAN PASSENGER COACHES.

The coaches are corridor bogie coaches on C.S.A.R. and C.G.R. Each compartment accommodates six passengers sitting, or four sleeping, a few of the C.G.R. 2nd class coaches accommodate 6 passengers sleeping in each compartment. N.G.R. passenger coaches have the same accommodation, but are not corridor.

APPENDIX II.

Payable by the WAR OFFICE.

No. _____ **H. Q.** _____

RAILWAY WARRANT for the use only of **OFFICERS,** Ladies of Q.A.I. Military Nursing Service, and the families of Officers enumerated in paragraph 339, Allowance Regulations, travelling on duty without Troops in the United Kingdom.

This Warrant must be presented to the Booking Clerk at the place where the holder is authorised to commence the journey, when a ticket will be issued in exchange.

Date _____ 19____

Station _____

Please issue _____ First Class $\frac{\text{single}}{\text{return}}$ journey ticket† *and* ticket for* _____ bicycle, from _____

to _____ at Military rates to bearer, travelling on duty, the fare to be paid by the War Office.

Signature of Issuing Officer _____

Rank and Corps _____

To be filled in by the Booking Clerk.

	Ordinary passenger fare. £ s. d.	Amount payable. £ s. d.
No. of Passenger Ticket		
No. of Bicycle Ticket		
From		
To	Ordinary bicycle rate.	
Route *via*		

_____ Booking Clerk.

_____ Station.

_____ Date.

* One or more.

† The words in italics should be struck out when bicycles are not taken for use on duty.

Not available for Families (except those enumerated in paragraph 339, Allowance Regulations), for soldier or civilian servants, or for horses. [P.T.O.

D

APPENDIX II—*continued.*

(Back of Warrant, Army Book 205.)

Particulars of Service.

To be filled in by the issuing Officer for classification in the Cash Account.

Rank.	Name.	Unit.	Nature of Duty.	Authority for journey.
1.				
2.				
3.				

Reasons for adopting other than the most direct railway or steamship route (*see* Allowance Regulations).

[P.T.O.

	Nature of Duty.	Authority for journey.
1.		
2.		
3.		

APPENDIX II—*continued.* Army Book 206.

RAILWAY WARRANT (except for Journeys between two Irish Stations).

This Warrant must be presented to the Booking Clerk at the Station where the holder is authorised to commence the Journey, when a Railway Ticket will be issued in exchange.

Dated at _____ 19___

The Directors of the _____ Railway Company are hereby requested to provide conveyance from
_____ Station to _____ [_____] *via* _____ ,
for the undermentioned party, the Fare to be defrayed by the War Office.
(*Signature*) _____ (*Rank and Corps*) _____

The endorsement of the Warrant should be fully completed.

No. of Warrant.	If not under Route, state below whether for a *RECRUIT for the LINE, or SPECIAL RESERVE; for a Man ON DISCHARGE, or ON TRANSFER to ARMY RESERVE; or for what other service.	This Warrant is †NOT chargeable against the public.
No. _____	* Inserting place of Attestation } _____	*Initials of Issuing Officer* } _____ † If the cost is chargeable to the public, strike out "NOT" and initial

	Number to be conveyed. To be filled in by the Issuer of the Warrant, all blanks being crossed through.			To be filled in by Railway Company.	
	At ⅓ Ordinary Passenger Fare. (WORDS).	At ½ Ordinary Passenger Fare. (WORDS).	Equal to the undermentioned number of Passengers at full Ordinary Passenger Fares.	Ordinary Passenger Fare.	Amount payable.
Officers, 1st Class—Officers					
Warrant Officers and their families, by 2nd Class when available, otherwise by 3rd Class.‡ { Warrant Officers .... Wives .... Children of 12 years of age and upwards—*at fares for adults* .... ** Do. of 3 years and under 12 —*half fares for adults* TOTAL					
Non-Commissioned Officers and Men, 3rd Class.‡ { Men .... Women .... Children of 12 years of age and upwards—*at fares for adults* .... ** Do. between 3 and 12— *half fares for adults* .... TOTAL					
TOTAL FOR OFFICERS, MEN, &c.					

		§Weight, including contents.		†† Horses.		To be filled in by the Railway Company.		
	Description.	No.	Tons.	cwts.	qrs.	In horse boxes.	In cattle trucks.	Mileage.	Rate.	Amount.
Guns and Limbers ...										
Wagons and Limbers										
Vehicles										
					§ Total Weight of Guns, &c., as per margin.					
					Tons.	cwts.	qrs.			
					Bicycles	No.				
							GRAND TOTAL .... £			

** Children under 3 years of age will not be included in the numbers making up the first 125 persons.
†† All Horses, except Officers' Chargers, will be sent in Cattle trucks, except when allowed to go in horse boxes under the King's Regulations.
‡ When a steamship journey is included, the class to which the passengers are entitled should be stated, if it differs from that by railway.
§ The weight of baggage and stores not packed in Army Vehicles must be excluded, separate forms to be used for traffic not so packed.

Particulars to be filled in by the Booking Clerk. {
No. of Ticket issued in exchange _____ Date _____
Route *via* _____
Amount _____
Booking Clerk, _____ Station.

Counter-signature of *Official representing Railway Company* _____

Any alteration in the Warrant which may be absolutely necessary must be verified by the Signature of the person who makes the alteration.

APPENDIX II—*continued.*
(Back of Warrant, Army Book 206.)

* EXTRACT from Route No.   given at

the   day of   19

By Order of

and signed by

___

of †

and

to proceed from   to

via   for the purpose of

return

I hereby Certify the above is a true Extract of the Route quoted above.

(*Signature of Issuer of Warrant*) _____

* If an extract cannot be given (as in cases of covering Routes) the nature of the duty should be stated.
† Here insert particulars of Corps.

___

Reasons for adopting a Route other than the cheapest.... {

___

Account in which credit will be given for any excess or in- }
admissible charges; and amount of the same.   }

___

Form to be filled in by the Issuer of the Warrant.

When the names of the party are too numerous, the name of the person in charge and the number (in words) of the men of each rank need only be entered in these columns.

Wives and families of Warrant Officers, Non-Com missioned Officers and Men on the MARRIED ROLL

Regiment or Corps.	Squadron, Battery or Company.	NAMES.	NAMES.	Children.	
				Sex.	Age.

APPENDIX II—*continued.*

Army Form P. 1904.

Army Baggage Consignment Note.

(To be retained by the Railway Company.)

The _____ Railway Station.

_____ Station.

Please {collect / receive} the undermentioned consignment of Baggage, the total charges for which will be paid on delivery at destination.

I certify that I am entitled, under the Allowance Regulations, to conveyance at the public expense for _____ cwts., which is chargeable at the statutory rate for Military Baggage. The remainder, being the excess beyond the weight authorized by regulation, is chargeable at the Railway Company's full ordinary rates

Signature of Owner.

_____ Rank and Corps.

_____ Date.

_____ Address.

Name and Address of Consignee.	Number and Description of Packages.	Weight.			
		Tons.	cwts.	qrs.	lbs.
		Total......			

NOTE.—(1.) To be used by individual officers and Warrant Officers not travelling under route.
(2.) Both parts of the form, when not otherwise directed, should be filled in as far as possible by the consigning officer before handing to the Railway Company.

(B 11089)

E

APPENDIX II—*continued.*

Army Baggage Consignment Note.

Army Form P. 1904.

(*To be returned to Consignee and ultimately retained by him.*)

Baggage of—

Rank _____

Name _____

Corps _____

To _____ Railway Company.

To be removed { From _____ To _____

Station.

Name and Address of Consignee.	No. and Description of Packages.	*Weight.				*Distance.		*Rate.		*Charges.			
		T.	C.	Q.	lbs.	No. of Miles.		Military.	Public.	Collection. £ s. d.	Carriage. £ s. d.	Delivery. £ s. d.	Total. £ s. d.
	Total.......												

Authorized by Army Regulations charged at statutory Rate for Military Baggage

Excess beyond weight authorized by Army Regulations, chargeable at ordinary public Rate ....

Total charge £

* To be completed as regards weight, distance, rate, and charges, by the Railway Company.

Received the above Amount

Name and Railway Co.

Station.

Date.

APPENDIX II—*continued*

RAILWAY WARRANT.

(*To be used only when a Vehicle Rate is charged.*)

This Warrant is NOT a railway ticket and must be exchanged for a ticket at the booking office. It is not to be used for parties numbering less than thirty unless they are necessarily accompanied by a large quantity of military baggage.

Date _____

The Directors of the _____ Railway Company are hereby requested to provide conveyance from__ _____ station to _____ viâ___ _____

_____ for the undermentioned troops with their guns, army vehicles and baggage, and to charge the cost thereof against the Army Ledger Account.

Signature _____ Rank and Corps _____

No. of Warrant.	No.	To be filled in by Railway Company.			
			No.	Rate.	Amount payable.
Officers					£ s. d.
Warrant officers, N.C.Os. and men					
Women		Railway passenger vehicles			
Children over 3 years		Other railway vehicles			
Camp followers		carrying passengers or			
		animals, guns, army			
Total passengers to receive ticket		vehicles and baggage ...			
Horses or transport animals		Initials of Railway Transport Officer certifying as to number of vehicles			
		Grand Total .... £			

Particulars to be filled in by the booking clerk
{ No. and date of ticket issued in exchange _____
{ Route viâ _____
{ Amount _____
_____ booking clerk _____ station.

Counter signature of official representing Railway Company _____

(SEE BACK.)

APPENDIX II—*continued.*

(Back of Railway Warrant used when a Vehicle Rate is charged.)

The following particulars of the troops travelling on this Warrant are to be filled in by the Issuer of Warrant.

Regiment or Corps.	Squadron, Battery, or Company.	No. of Officers.	No. of Warrant Officers, N.C.Os and Men.	No. of Camp Followers.	No. of Women.	No. of Children.	No. of Horses or Transport Animals.	No. of Guns.	No. of Army Vehicles.	Remarks.

APPENDIX III.

STANDARD FORM OF REPORT ON AN EXISTING RAILWAY.

Name of Country.

Report on the A. B. Railway.

General Map of the Country.

Showing all railway systems, each separate system being marked with the initials of its name after the style of the English Railway Clearing House map.

Map of the A. B. Railway.

Showing mileages of all principal towns and branch lines, showing also all rivers of any size crossed, and rivers and ranges of hills in vicinity.

Railways projected or under construction to be shown, the notation denoting state of progress, *i.e.*, surveyed, formation complete, permanent way laid.

The section of the A. B. line (rail level only not ground level) to reduced scale, heights exaggerated to distances as recorded in the office of the chief engineer of the railway.

NUMBER of Tracks.

Mileage.	Track.	Mileage.	Track.
0 to 52	Three tracks	Branch to A. town	Double
52 110	Double	,, B. ,, ...	Single
110 400	Single	&c.	
&c.	&c.		&c.

Portion electrified. on $\left\{ \begin{array}{c} \text{overhead} \\ \text{third rail} \end{array} \right\}$ system.

Mile 0 to 52 steam and electricity traction
Branch to A. town steam and electricity traction.
All remainder steam only.

RULING Gradient in Decimal of a Foot per 100 Feet including Compensation for Curvature or in a Fraction.

Mileage.					Ruling Gradient.
0 to 100	....	....	....	....	·7
100 230	. ..	....	....	....	1 ·1
230 400	....	....	....	....	2 ·0

APPENDIX III—*continued*.

MAXIMUM Curvature Main Line in Degrees or in Feet Radius.

Mileage.					Maximum Curvature.
0 to 130	....	....	....	....	9°
130 250	....	....	....	....	12°
250 400	....	....	....	....	20°

NUMBER of Trains actually Running in Busiest Times.

Mileage.	Passengers.	Goods.	Total.	Average* Speed Passenger.	Average* Speed Goods.
0 to 52 ...	10 through ...	20 through ...	30	28 miles per hour	15 miles per hour
	10 local ...	10 local ...	20	15 miles per hour	10 miles per hour
52 to 110 &c. ...	&c.	&c.	&c.	&c.	&c.

* Including stoppages.

Skeleton Types of Locomotives.

Showing number of wheels coupled, bogies or ponies additional to driving wheels, tender or tank engine, passenger or goods, diameter driving wheel, wheel base measurement, weight on each axle loaded, *vide* diagrams below. Water and coal capacity. (These drawings are kept in office of chief locomotive superintendent.) Nature of brake employed. Makers names and addresses.

Type A (Goods tender Engine).

State number available.

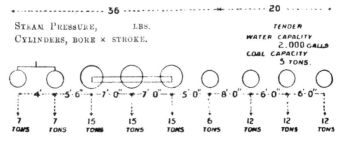

APPENDIX III—*continued.*

Type B (Passenger tender Engine).

&c.   &c.
&c.   &c.

Type C.

&c.   &c.

Type D.

Fuel.—Coal, oil or wood, where procured, situation and output of collieries, quality of fuel.

TRAIN LOADS of different type Locos., excluding weight of Locos., Tender and Caboose.

Ruling Gradient.	Type A Loco.		Type B Loco.		Type C Loco.		Type D Loco.	
	Gross Load.	Net Load.	Gross Load.	Net Load.	Gross Load.	Net Load.	Gross Load.	Net Load.
	Tons.	Tons.	Tons.	Tons.	Tons.	Tons.	Tons.	Tons.
1·1								
2·0								

Trucks.—Skeleton type drawings of main types, stating quantity of each type available, tare and load, whether sides and ends let down throughout, area of floor space, nature of brake, whether coupled throughout train and controlled from engine. Buffers side or centre, height above rail level and distance apart, nature of coupling. Particular attention to be paid to acquiring information as to the number of cattle trucks and number of long low-sided trucks. Capacity for men, horses, guns, vehicles.

Passenger Coaches.—Types not required, quantity only. Capacity for men.

Diagram of loading gauge on railway.

If rolling stock is not made in railway shops give names of principal manufacturers.

APPENDIX III—continued.

STATIONS and Crossing Places, Distance Apart, and all Particulars.

On many lines stations are divided into classes, and a type exists for each class, in which case the most of the undermentioned information is best shown by type drawings.

Mileage.	Name of Station.	Number of Loop Sidings.	Number of Dead Ends.	Truck Capacity.*	Turntable, seating Diameter.	Triangle.	Lighting.	Wagon loading Platform, feet run.	Telegraph Instrument.†	Telephone on Trunk Line.	Phonopore.	Block Instrument.‡	Coal Depot.§	Water Storage, gallons.‖	Goods Shed accommodation in square feet.	Engine Changing Depot for Engines.	Running Shed, length of pit.	Repairing Shed, yes or no.	Engine Pit without Shed, feet run.	District Store, square feet.	Number of Home Signals.	Number of Distant Signals.	Number of Starting Signals.	Number of Points interlocked with Signals.	Rodding or Wire to Points.	Signal Lever Box, yes or no.	Point Lever Box, yes or no.	Power for Signal working.¶
0	A. Town																											
5	B. Town																											
7½	Crossing place, &c., &c.																											

* Number should denote equivalent of short four-wheel trucks or vans, bogies be counted as two.   † State nature of Instrument Morse Recorder, single needle or other kind.   ‡ State nature of Block Instrument (Tablet staff, &c.) and name of maker.   § State quantity in tons, whether discharged from overhead bins with hoist thereto, or from wood stage in tip trucks, or in sacks by hand, &c., denoting Bins by B., Tip Trucks by T., Hand by H.   ‖ For details of water supply see separate table.   ¶ E. for Electric power, P. for Pneumatic, H. for Hand Power, T. for Track Circuit.

APPENDIX III—*continued.*

Permanent Way (state the Gauge).—If any alterations in any particulars on different section, state the mileages where alterations commence.

Double headed ⎫ lb. rail, length, height, inches (if possible,
Flat bottomed ⎭ drawing of section of rail).

Wood ⎫
Iron
Steel
Wood, creosoted ⎬ Sleepers, length, breadth, depth.
  (hard or soft)
Iron pot
Steel pot ⎭

Chairs, yes or no.
Chairplates, yes or no.
Coach screws, length, diameter, dimension of a square head.
Iron dog spikes, length, breadth.
Trenails, length, diameter.
Steel keys.
Ballast, nature of, depth, condition.
Angles of main line turn-outs.
Fixed structure gauge.

TUNNELS.

From Mile.	To Mile.	Wood, Brick, Stone Lining or Unlined.

APPENDIX III—continued.

Bridges of 30′ Span and Over.

Mileage.	Number of Spans.	Length of Clear Span and Height " "	P. Plate Girder. L. Lattice Girder. T. Timber Girder. T. I. Timber beam.	TH. through span. D. Deck span.	Total length of Bridge.	Nature of Abutments.	Number of Stone Piers.	Number of Cylinder Piers.	Number of Iron Trestles.	Number of Wood Trestles.	Number of Pile Piers.	Number of Crib Piers.	Other Piers.	Number of Deep Channels.	Width of Deep Channels.	Depth of Deep Channels at Low Water.	Average Depth outside Deep Channels at Low Water.	Flood Period.	Difference between High and Low Water.	Height from Low Water to Rail Level.	Nature of River Bed.	Speed of Current in Miles per Hour.	Nature of Banks.	Possibility of making Low Level Deviations.

Good timber for bridging or for sleepers can be cut at

Stone quarries exist at

Mark with * bridges which should be specially guarded owing to special conditions which would cause much delay in reconstruction if damaged.

APPENDIX III—continued.

WATER SUPPLY.

Mileage.	Name of Station (if any).	Storage in Station, gallons.	Number of Storage Tanks.	Number of Engine, Water Columns, or Hose Attachments.	Source of Supply: Well (depth and description).	Dam (gallons stored).	Artificial Reservoir (gallons stored).	River.	Lake.	Pond from Springs, &c., &c.	Pumped or by Gravitation.	Pumping Power, hand, wind, steam, electrical, gasolene, &c., &c.	Name of Pump.	Diameter Suction Pipe.	Diameter Delivery Pipe.

State if any sections of the Line are particularly waterless, necessitating tank trucks being run behind engine and tender. If so, how many tank trucks on each line?

APPENDIX III—*continued.*

WORKSHOPS.

Name of Station.	Loco. Shops, Engineering Shops, or Telegraph Shops.	Nature of Shop, i.e., Erecting, Machine, &c.	Length.	Breadth.	Power, Electrical or Steam Bracket. All Shops driven from the same source.	Horse-power or Kilowatts available.	Lighting.	Particulars of Machinery.

or Area.

If possible note the quantities and the thicknesses of steel plate available in Workshop or General Stores.

APPENDIX III—*continued.*

Stores.—State where central stores are located, and, if possible, how many months' supply supposed to be stored there; also situation and sizes of district stores, brickfields, &c. Situations of any reserve stocks of timber, sleepers, rails, bricks; either on the railway or near it; facilities for loading and unloading.

Sea-port at Railway Base or Terminus.—Wharfage front, with or without railway track, cranage, tonnage and draught or shipping accommodated. Effect, if any, of tides or frost.

Piers, nature of, with or without rail track, cranage, effect of tides, shipping accommodated.

Necessity for lighters; number of lighters, weight and cubic content of largest package taken by lighters.

Unskilled Labour of the Country.—Races of unskilled labour, efficiency as labourers, any customs peculiar and necessary to follow such as organization in gangs under headmen, when native. Numbers available, sources of supply, agents to procure. Current market wage.

Skilled Labour.—Any skilled labour not hostile which can be trusted.

Information regarding the internal organization of the personnel should be given in the case of English owned railways or railways in English colonies whose staff may be expected to work the railway in time of war.

In such cases information should be given on the following points :—

(i) Supreme authority, *i.e.*, government, shareholders, local boards, &c.

(ii) Where the manager of the whole line, and heads of the various departments are stationed.

(iii) Extent of each district into which the line is divided, and headquarters of each locomotive, traffic, and engineer district offices.

Rates.—If the army possesses any special agreement for rates over the railway, quote it, otherwise give tables of public passenger fares, rough goods rate and coal rate.

APPENDIX IV.

APPROXIMATE BULK OF MILITARY STORES.

Hay (compressed)	....	....	116 cubic feet per ton.
Biscuits	....	....	112 ,, ,,
Bran (compressed)	....	....	42 ,, ,,
Flour	....	....	80 ,, ,,
Oats	....	....	80 ,, ,,
Sugar	....	....	60 ,, ,,
Preserved meat	....	....	67 to 75 ,, ,,

Fodder, not compressed, may be taken at about 170 to 180 cubic feet per ton.

Ordnance stores may be taken at 60 cubic feet per ton and with them full loads are generally obtainable.

APPENDIX IV—continued.

The following are examples of actual loading in Cape Government Stock during the South African War :—

CARRYING CAPACITY OF ROLLING STOCK.

	Long Bogie.	Short Bogie.	Covered Bogie.	Sheep Bogie.
Full capacity ...	Lbs. 45,000	Lbs. 25,000	Lbs. 22,500	Lbs. 22,500

ACTUAL AVERAGE LOADING.

Consignment.	Long Bogie.		Short Bogie.		Covered Bogie.		Sheep Bogie.	
	Weight.	Per cent. of full.	Weight.	Per cent. of full.	Weight.	Per cent. of full.	Weight.	Per cent. of full.
Hay	22,000	48·8	18,000	72	21,000	93·3	11,000	48·8
Biscuits ...	22,000	48·8	15,000	60	18,000	80	13,000	58·2
Bran ...	21,000	46·6	15,000	60	18,000	80	12,000	53·5
Meal ...	40,000	88·8	22,000	88	22,000	97·7	18,000	80
Oats ...	42,000	93·2	20,000	80	22,000	97·7	18,000	80
Sugar ...	45,000	100	25,000	100	22,500	100	22,500	100

APPENDIX V.

TRUCK SPACE TAKEN UP BY ARMY VEHICLES.

Guns.

	Weight.				Width over all.		Length without Limber.		Limber.		Length required in Truck.	
	Gun and Carriage.		Limber.									
	tons.	cwts.	tons.	cwts.	ft.	in.	ft.	in.	ft.	in.	ft.	in.
13-pr. Q.F.		19½		13	6	3	12	2	5	3	13	0
18-pr. Q.F.	1	5		15	6	3	13	8	5	4½	14	0
5-in. B.L. Howitzer	1	3¾		22½	6	2	9	3	5	6	15	1
60-pr. B.L.	4	11		16½	6	6½	21	7	7	7	32	4
Maxim Gun I.F. Carriage III		9¾		....		....	10	3		....	10	3

APPENDIX V—*continued*.

Ammunition Wagons.

	Weight.		Width over all.	Length without Limber.	Limber.	Length required in Truck.
	Without Limber.	Limber.				
	tons. cwts.	tons. cwts.	ft. in.	ft. in.	ft. in.	ft. in.
13-pr. Q.F. ...	15¾	14¾	6 3	7 11	6 1	14 0
18-pr. Q.F. ...	18¾	17¾	6 3	8 0	6 0	14 0
5-in. B.L., Mark II ...	1 9¼	19½	6 2	8 4	6 9	15 1
60-pr. B.L. (converted Q.F. 15-pr. wagons) ...	1 9¾	18¼	6 0	8 3½	5 11	14 2½

APPENDIX V —continued.

Wagons and Carts.

Nature of Vehicle.	Length taken up in truck, shaft or pole detached.	Additional length for second similar vehicle.	Width over all.
Wagon, G.S., Mark IX to X* ...	13' 7"	13' 3"	6' 4"
Wagon, ambulance, Mark VI ...	13' 10"	13' 10"	7' 0½"
Wagon, pontoon, R.E., Marks IV* and V	17' 4"	16' 4"	6' 8"
Length of pontoon on wagon ...	21' 0"	21' 0"	6' 8"
Wagon, cable, telegraph and limber, R.E.	16' 1"	16' 1"	6' 2½"
Wagon, limbered, G.S., Mark I ...	13' 9"	13' 3"	6' 4"
Cart, forage (shafts on) ...	13' 10½"	0' 3"	6' 1"
Cart, Maltese (shafts on), Mark V and V*	12' 6½"	0' 0"	6' 1"
Cart, water tank (ditto), Mark II*	13' 11"	1' 1"	6' 1"
Cart, tool, R.E. (ditto), Mark II	10' 9"	6' 0"	6' 2¼"

APPENDIX VI.

Table showing Composition of Railway Trains required for Units* at War Strength with British Rolling Stock.

	Standard Compositions.																				Special Compositions.							
	A.	B.	C.	D.	E.	F.	G.	H.	K.	L.	M.	N.	O.	P.	Q.	R.	S.	T.	U.	V.	Hd. Qrs. Cav. Division, Hd. Qrs. Cav. Divnl. Art. and Hd. Qrs. Cav. Divnl. A.S.C.	Hd. Qrs. Cav. Brigade and I Signal Troop, not allotted to a Cav. Division.	Hd. Qrs. Inf. Division and Hd. Qrs. Divnl. Artillery.	Hd. Qrs. Divnl. R.E., Hd. Qrs. and No. 1 Section Divnl. Signal Company.	Mtd. Brigade Hd. Qrs. and Section of a Yeomanry and Machine Gun Regt. (T.F.)	Hd. Qrs. of a Division, and Hd. Qrs. Divnl. Artillery (T.F.)	Hd. Qrs. of 3 Infantry Brigades (T.F.)
Compartments ...	17	21	15	14	18	17	66	10	29	20	8	8	10	8	9	16	11	30	16	18	24	13	16	13	13	16	16
Horse boxes ...																											
Cattle trucks ...	12	24	16	13	9	11	6	14	12	6	12	5	4	6	7	8	14	20	8		9	11	7	10	10	6	5
Vehicle trucks ...	9	5	10	14	12	16	8	15	13	8	17	4	8	6	11	6	19	8	4	15	5	6	6	12	5	4	6
Brake vans ...	2	2	2	2	2	2	2	2	2	2	2	2	2	2	2	2	2	2	2	2	2	2	2	2	2	2	2
Total Railway Vehicles ...	26	34	31	31	26	32	26	33	31	19	18	16	18	19	16	22	17	34	29	28	30	22	28	24	29	29	23

* Not including details left at the Base or first reinforcements.

RAILWAY TRAINS FOR 1 CAVALRY DIVISION.

Unit.	Train Load.	No. of Trains.	Composition.
Headquarters of Division (less motor-cars), Headquarters Cavalry Divisional Artillery and Headquarters Cavalry Divisional A.S.C.	....	1	Special
4 Cavalry Brigades (12 Cavalry Regiments)	Headquarters of Brigade and 1 Signal Troop	4	N
4 Signal Troops	Headquarters of Regiment and Machine-Gun Section	12	T
	1 Squadron of Cavalry	36	B
Divisional Artillery—	Half Battery	8	C
2 Horse Artillery Brigades	Brigade Headquarters and "C" Sub-section Ammunition Column	2	D
	"A" and "B" Sub-sections Ammunition Column	2	D
	Ammunition Column Headquarters and "F" Sub-section....	2	D
Divisional Engineers—	Headquarters Bridging Detachment and 1 Troop	1	D
1 Field Squadron	3 Troops	1	T
Divisional Signal Service—	Headquarters "A" and "B" Troops	1	D
1 Signal Squadron	"C" and "D" Troops....	1	A
Divisional Medical Units— 4 Cavalry Field Ambulances	1 Cavalry Field Ambulance	4	F
	Total Railway Trains	75	....

APPENDIX VI—*continued.*

RAILWAY TRAINS FOR 1 INFANTRY DIVISION.

Unit.	Train Load.	No. of Trains.	Composition. Special
Headquarters of the Division and Headquarters Divisional Artillery	.....	1	O
3 Infantry Brigades	Brigade Headquarters and a Section Divisional Signal Company	3	G
	Headquarters of Battalion (less Major, Quartermaster-Serjeant, Transport Serjeant, Pioneers, Half Stretchers, Bearers, 2 S.A.A. Carts, 1 Water Cart, 1 Tool Wagon, Spare Horses, Major's Bâtman and Horse, 3 R.A.M.C. personnel, and 2 Train Wagons) and 2 Companies of Infantry.	12	
	Remainder of Headquarters ... ... Machine Gun Section ... ... 2 Companies of Infantry	12	G
Divisional Mounted Troops— 1 Cavalry Squadron	1 Cavalry Squadron	1	B
Divisional Artillery— 3 Field Artillery Brigades	Brigade Headquarters, "B" Sub-section Ammunition Column and 1 Train Wagon	3	D
	"A" and "C" Sub-sections Ammunition Column ...	3	D
	"D" and "E" Sub-sections Ammunition Column and 1 Train Wagon	3	E
	Half Battery and 1 Train Wagon	18	D

1 Field Artillery (Howitzer) Brigade	Headquarters " A " Sub-section Ammunition Column and 1 Train Wagon	1	D
	" B " and " C " Sub-sections Ammunition Column and 1 Train Wagon	1	D
1 Heavy Artillery Battery and Ammunition Column	Half Battery	6	D
	Half Battery and Half Ammunition Column ...	2	D
1 Divisional Ammunition Column ...	Headquarters and No. 4 Section (Heavy portion) ...	1	E
	Half Section (No. 1, 2 or 3)	6	H
	No. 4 Section (Howitzer portion) ...	1	D
Divisional Engineers— Headquarters, 2 Field Companies and Headquarters and No. 1 Section Divisional Signal Company	Headquarters Divisional Engineers and Headquarters and No. 1 Section Divisional Signal Company	1	Special
	1 Field Company	2	K
Divisional Transport and Supply Unit— Divisional Train (less Transport with Units)	Headquarters, Headquarters Company and No. 2 Company	1	K
	Nos. 3 and 4 Companies	1	E
Divisional Medical Units— 3 Field Ambulance	Half Field Ambulance	6	Q
Total Railway Trains		85	...

APPENDIX VI—continued.

RAILWAY TRAINS FOR OTHER REGULAR UNITS.

Unit.	Train Load.	No. of Trains.	Composition.
Headquarters of a Cavalry Brigade and 1 Signal Troop, not allotted to a Cavalry Division	……	1	Special
Headquarters of a General Headquarters Signal Co., and Headquarters of an Army Headquarters Signal Co. (less mechanical transport)	……	1	L
Air-Line Section (less 3-ton lorry) …… Cable Section …… ……	} Two Sections ……	1	A
Wireless Section …… …… ……	Wireless Section ……	1	P
1 Bridging Train …… …… ……	One-fifth Train ……	5	M
Army Troops Train (less transport with units and motor-car)	……	1	L (less 9 compartments)

APPENDIX VI—*continued.*

RAILWAY TRAINS FOR A TERRITORIAL FORCE DIVISION.

Unit.	Train Load.	No. of Trains.	Composition.
Headquarters of Division and Headquarters of Divisional Artillery	…	1	Special
3 Infantry Brigades	3 Brigade Headquarters	1	Special
	Half Infantry Battalion	24	G
Divisional Artillery—			
Headquarters and 3 R.F.A. Brigades	Brigade Headquarters and Half Battery	3	D
	Half Battery Artillery	15	A
	Half Ammunition Column	6	H
Field Artillery (Howitzer) Brigade	Headquarters and Half Battery	1	D
	Three-quarter Battery Artillery	2	D
	Ammunition Column	1	K (less 18 compartments)
Heavy Artillery Battery and Ammunition Column	Three-quarter Battery Artillery	1	D
	Quarter Battery Artillery and Ammunition Column	1	E (plus 1 vehicle truck)
Divisional Engineers—			
2 Field Companies	1 Field Company	2	K
1 Divisional Signal Company	Headquarters Divisional Engineers and 1 Signal Company	1	R

APPENDIX VI—continued.

RAILWAY TRAINS FOR A TERRITORIAL FORCE DIVISION—continued.

Unit.	Train Load.	Number of Trains.	Composition.
Yeomanry Regiment	Quarter Regiment	4	U
Divisional Transport and Supply Column (excluding Mechanical Transport.)	Quarter Transport and Supply Column	4	S (less 21 compartments)
3 Field Ambulances	1 Field Ambulance	3	S
	Total Railway Trains ...	70	...

RAILWAY TRAINS FOR A MOUNTED BRIGADE (T.F.).

Unit.	Train Load.	Number of Trains.	Composition.
Mounted Brigade Headquarters	Mounted Brigade Headquarters and Headquarters and Machine Gun Section of 1 Yeomanry Regiment	1	Special
	Headquarters and Machine Gun Section of 2 Yeomanry Regiments ...	1	T
3 Yeomanry Regiments	Squadron Yeomanry	9	U

			K A (less 10 compartments)	V
Horse Artillery Battery and Mounted Brigade Ammunition Column ... { Half Battery Ammunition Column	...	...	2 1	
Mounted Brigade Transport and Supply Column ... T. & S. Column complete	...	...	1	V
Mounted Brigade Field Ambulance ... 1 Field Ambulance	...	...	1	V
Total Railway Trains for a Mounted Brigade (T.F.) ...			16	...

NOTE.—The above tables are based on the following data, which are the average figures for British rolling stock :—

6 Officers to each compartment.

8 men to each compartment.

7 horses, unharnessed or unsaddled, to each cattle truck, except heavy draught, which are taken at 6 per truck.

3 Staff Officers chargers to each horse box.

1 four-wheeled vehicle, or 1 gun and limber, to each open truck, except 60-pr. guns and limbers, which are allowed 2 trucks ; and pontoons, which are allowed 3 trucks to 2 pontoons.

2 two-wheel vehicles to each open truck.

5 to 8 compartments to a coach.

These train loads may be considered normal for broad gauge railways in war. But the loads are, generally speaking, heavy, and though most of the railways in the United Kingdom could deal with them, it might be necessary even in this country to run some of the heavier loads in two portions over sections of lines where gradients are severe or on lines whose engines are light.

The above tables are based on War Establishments, Part I, 1914, except those for the Territorial Force, which are based on War Establishments, Part II, 1911.

G